Elementary

Creative Bulletin Boards

JOANNE G. HORNICK

Art for Mrs. Hornick's original boards
by Dan Dickas

Cover by Schon & Barber

Citation Press   New York   1969

For my mother and father

"How to Eat a Poem" by Eve Merriam, © 1964 by Eve Merriam from IT DOESN'T ALWAYS HAVE TO RHYME. Used by permission of Atheneum Publishers.

Excerpt from "Arithmetic" from COMPLETE POEMS by Carl Sandburg, copyright 1950 by Carl Sandburg. Reprinted by permission of Harcourt, Brace & World, Inc.

Library of Congress Catalog Card Number: 75-89470

Copyright © 1969 by Scholastic Magazines, Inc. This edition published by Citation Press, Professional Relations Division, Scholastic Magazines, Inc. Editorial Offices: 50 West 44th St., New York, N.Y. 10036.

Printed in the U.S.A.

Second printing, 1972

Contents

Creating Effective Bulletin Boards

About Bulletin Boards   Today's ad-conscious students respond enthusiastically to visual media. Posters, banners, and signs often decorate the walls of their rooms. The same elements that attract them — humor and striking design — can be equally effective in the classroom. The bulletin boards in this book will provide informal reinforcement to lessons, motivation for new subjects, and new ways to display students' work. Also, the lively look of the boards will stimulate freer response from students.

These boards were designed with both teacher and students in mind. Because a teacher's time is limited, the boards are kept uncomplicated and the directions simple. The following few pages suggest some techniques and materials for bulletin-board construction so that students and teachers can create and illustrate their own ideas.

Try Different Linings   A lining can make the most ordinary board appealing. Try a plaid behind homework papers, bright crumpled tissue to show off tests, or newspaper to back compositions. *Any* simple scheme benefits from a gay lining: gift wrap, foil, cellophane, self-adhesive paper, a fabric or wallpaper remnant, or a paper table cloth. (Party cloths come in many colors and designs.)

When the display is colorful and busy, keep to a simple lining: shelf, crepe, or construction paper, oaktag, felt, or burlap.

If the lining material does not cover the entire board, leave some of the cork visible — it's an interesting contrast. A frame of complementary paper, or a paper fringe can give the display a finished look. For fringe, cut a two-inch strip of crepe paper and cut thin strips one and one-half inches deep. Staple the fringe along the top and bottom of the lining.

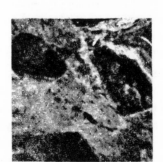

Vary the Composition   Shown above are a few easy design concepts: balanced large and small elements; combinations of circles, squares, rectangles, and triangles; papers marched across at an angle; symmetry and asymmetry. Each board in your room can have its own personality with different colors, textures, and layouts. The keynote is variety.

Try setting a part of the board you want to emphasize at a different level or angle from the rest. A message or title receives extra attention if placed in an unexpected position.

Attractive Letters Are Easy

Handmade letters are more attractive than perfect packaged letters — which are dull to look at, expensive, and too small. Here's an easy way to make cutout letters:

Don't try to make perfect letters. Just draw them naturally, using the printed alphabet. A combination of capital and small letters is more interesting than all capitals.

Always draw the letter with a felt marker. When you cut them out, this will leave a dark outline around each letter. Even if the letters are unequal in size and not symmetrical, they will look as if they were done that way purposely. The right outlining color adds a surprising touch to the letters.

Other attractive letterings include: string or yarn stapled into cursive writing (below), fluffy cotton stuck to Elmer's-glue-writing (for winter scenes), letters cut from newspapers or magazines (glued to construction paper to reinforce them); glitter-accented letters; letters made from pipe cleaners, felt or other fabrics, cardboard, plain or painted popsicle sticks, wallpaper, or self-adhesive paper (just cut out letters and tear off backing). To spark a plain board, ask each student to bring in a different letter made of anything he chooses.

Make It 3-D with Springs . . .

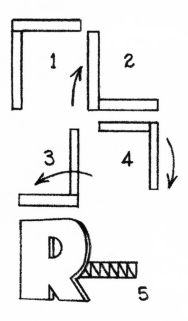

It's easy to enliven a board just by making letters, pictures, papers, or objects three-dimensional. Springs give a bouncy effect, and students can make them. Cut strips of construction paper the width needed to support the letter. Tape two strips together at a right angle. Fold one over the other until the spring is completed. Tape it to the back of the letter or paper and then staple it to the board.

An especially nice idea is a fall, winter, or spring display beautifully decorated with student-made leaves, snowflakes, or flowers, each one backed by a spring. The result is a 3-D leaf-or-snowfall or bunches of colorful bouncy flowers to accentuate students' seasonal compositions or poetry.

. . . and Things

Other provocative 3-D effects can be obtained by attaching real items to the board, such as product boxes and wrappers, play money, small toys, and artificial flowers. This is a great way to strengthen students' involvement in the board.

Another way to make your board 3-D is to mount art, papers, titles and so forth on small, flat cereal boxes (the kind that come in a variety pack) or on paper loops, to make them stand away from the board. This is an excellent way to emphasize messages and titles.

Construction paper art can easily be made 3-D by raising part of it when stapling it to the board. For example, instead of stapling a paper branch or stem flat, leave a ripple in it.

Add a "Take-One" Folder

Attaching a Take-One folder increases a board's value as a center of independent activities. The exercise tucked into the folder follows up the lesson motivated by the board. It's perfect for students who finish their regular work early since it requires no help or explanation from the teacher. Giving "extra credit" for completed take-one assignments is a good incentive; but the fact that it's part of an attractive bulletin board also makes the idea of doing the independent work more exciting for the students.

Cut the tab-side of a manila folder horizontally, leaving about two-thirds of it.

Divide the piece cut off into four strips. Staple two to each side to hold the folder together (just loosely enough so that papers can be tucked inside).

Cover the front with construction paper, using glue or staples.

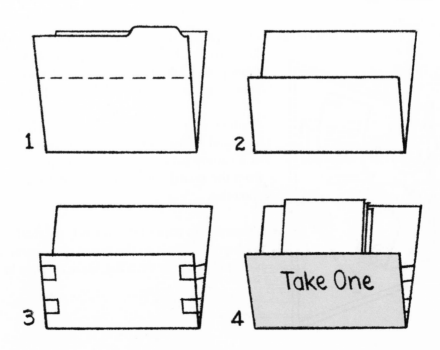

Even Children Can Make Large Figures . . .

It's good to involve the children in making boards whenever possible. Sometimes two or three can plan and execute a board themselves — sketching its layout on paper for your approval first. The hardest thing for children is drawing large figures for a board. You can help them by roughing out lightly in pencil the head, body, and feet — or just sketching horizontal lines to indicate the limits of size.

Children also enjoy constructing "collage people" of simple construction paper shapes — circles, triangles, rectangles — with scraps of cloth glued on for clothes, and yarn hair.

. . . and Enlarge Maps and Designs

One way of doing a large map, design, or other picture is to project it onto a big sheet of paper with an overhead or opaque projector — or even a slide projector — and have the children draw around the projected image with pencil or marker.

Reading

Would You Believe... Designed to stimulate pleasure reading, this board also involves number reading. Play money and a real paperback book make the board fun to look at, and the humorous message will bring a light touch into the classroom.

You'll need:

A lining for the board (pastel)

The message, "Would you believe . . ." (hot-pink marker)

Play money from the five-and-ten

A large drawing of a boy reading (Charlie Brown is a popular character, and many students can draw him.)

A paperback book (Staple it to the board by its back cover. A rubber band around all but the front cover will keep it from falling open.)

Teacher is foreign spy...

Scared old lady lives in haunted house...

What is not mysterious but has many mysteries???

Answer

Clues to mysterious doll in old diary...

Mysterious old letters vanish...

Dark swamp hides deserted house...

Ghost of ten-year-old boy appears...

Ancient curse brings evil and death...

Mystery Riddle   The answer to the riddle is "The School Library."

Here is a chance to display book jackets or paperbacks (ones your library owns) with a brief, mysterious clue to the plot of each book. A schedule of the library hours should also appear under the flap.

You'll need:

A lining for the board (green)

The riddle, "What Is Not Mysterious . . ." (green marker on yellow paper)

Mysterious phrases about the books, and an "Answer" flap (green marker on orange paper)

The riddle answer, "The School Library," and a copy of the school library schedule (Have a student copy them in black marker on white paper. Staple them under the "Answer" flap.)

Book jackets — librarians often keep them — or paperback books (Staple paperbacks to the board by their back covers. Rubber bands around all but the front cover will keep them from falling open.)

4 Times When you should not read for fun!

1

2

3

4

4 Times When You Should Not Read for Fun

Negative statements about reading always seem to arouse student interest because they are always being urged to read. The answers are humorous and meant to underscore the fun of recreational reading.

You'll need:

A lining for the board (an interesting texture)

Cutout letters for "4 Times When" (hot pink)

The message, "you <u>should not</u> read for fun!" (Match the color of the cutout letters.)

Four flaps numbered 1, 2, 3, 4 (hot-pink marker on white paper)

A message to staple under each flap (type or print):

flap number one: You should not read for fun when you don't feel like having fun. (But you <u>always</u> like fun. What a silly reason!)

flap number two: You should not read for fun if you are in charge of catching an elephant that escaped from the zoo. If an elephant escapes, don't read for fun. Just try to catch him. (Try reading him a nice story. He will listen to it and follow you right back to his cage.)

flap number three: Another good time not to read for fun is in the middle of Mrs. (teacher's name) social-studies lesson. Oh, why is reading so much fun during her social-studies lesson?

flap number four: The best time not to read for fun is when you told your mother you would do the dishes. But reading is so much fun when you know you should be doing something else!

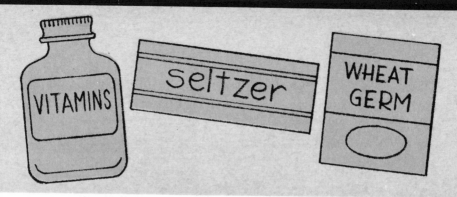

Friends, feeling bored? Nothing is any fun? Should you try vitamins, seltzer, or wheat germ? Or should you try an interesting, exciting, juicy, suspenseful, adventurous, eye-catching, heart-beating, breath-taking book?!!

Advertisement for Reading

This advertisement for reading draws upon the familiar cliches of television commercials. Children will especially like seeing the real boxes of products displayed on the board. They might even enjoy writing their own commercials for reading.

You'll need:

A lining for the board (green)

The "ad" (green marker on white paper)

Empty boxes of cereals, seltzer tablets, and vitamins to thumb-tack or staple to the board.

Grammar and Punctuation

Tadpoles or Apostrophes

tadpole

apostrophe

Which do you use to make contractions?
Apostrophes, of course! An apostrophe looks
like a tadpole, but it won't turn into a frog!

Take One

can't = can not
isn't = is not
won't = will not
shouldn't = should not
aren't = are not
Croak!

Tadpoles or Apostrophes While the class is studying contractions, this board humorously reminds them to use an apostrophe and displays some common contractions.

A study guide or self-quiz can be tucked into the Take-One pocket (in this case the frog himself) to provide an independent seat-work activity. (See example exercise, page 76.)

You'll need:

A lining for the board (chartreuse)

Cutout letters for "Tadpoles or Apostrophes" (dark green)

The message, "Which do you use . . ." (dark-green marker)

Two identical drawings of a tadpole and an apostrophe, labeled (black marker on white paper)

A big spotted frog labeled "Take One," leaving the top unstapled so the mimeographed quiz can be tucked in behind the frog (a green frog with darker green spots)

A conversation balloon containing several contractions that trouble your class (black marker on medium-green paper)

The Homymonsters

These words are monsters! They love to confuse you. But if you learn these horrible homonyms once, they'll never bother you again.

your - belonging to you
you're - you are
their - belonging to them
they're - they are
there - in that place

Take One

The Homymonsters This board can introduce a lesson on homonyms, or it can serve as a review or reminder. The hideous-but-funny monsters popping out from the board should appeal to the students.

Independent seat-work activities related to homonyms can be tucked into the Take-One pocket. (See example exercise, page 77.)

You'll need:

A lining for the board (orange)

Cutout letters for "The Homymonsters" (dark green)

The message "These words are monsters . . ." and the homonyms list (dark-green or black marker)

A Take-One folder (dark green or black. See instructions, page 11.)

Two or three large monster heads (Have students make them of construction paper or other materials. A contest for the best monster heads might be fun. Mount the heads on paper springs so they'll pop out from the board and jiggle a bit. See instructions, page 10.)

The 4 Types of Sentences

1. Statement - There is a hippopotamus.
2. Question - Is there a hippopotamus?
3. Exclamation - What a huge hippopotamus!
4. Command - Get that hippopotamus out of here!

Do Not Pet the Hippopotamus!

The 4 Types of Sentences

With a little humor, the four types of sentences are illustrated here. You might add the words "hippopotamus," "statement," "question," "exclamation," and "command" to your weekly spelling list.

You'll need:

A lining for the board (white or yellow)

The title and types of sentences (the title in brown marker, the types of sentences in green)

A "Do not pet the hippopotamus!" sign (brown lettering on white oaktag, mounted on a brown construction-paper "stake")

A hippopotamus (Draw or have a student draw it on dark-gray or brown construction paper, then cut it out.)

Grass and a couple of flowers (Sketch them in with markers or make them of construction paper. Plastic flowers will add a 3-D element.)

26

My teacher said to write down all the uses a dictionary has. I did, and she crossed out every one. Some teacher!

seat raiser
foot rest
book end
step stool
door stop
paper weight
flower presser
first base

definitions
pronunciations
antonyms and synonyms
parts of speech
weights and measures
countries and capitals
biographical information
word origins
signs and symbols

Dictionary Uses This board can motivate a dictionary unit or simply remind students of the various uses of their dictionaries.

You'll need:

A lining for the board (white)

The message "My teacher said . . ." and lists (Print the message across the top and the student's list in dark blue. In red, cross out the student's list and list the real uses in cursive writing — as if the student's list had been corrected in red by his teacher.)

A boy with baseball cap and glove and dictionary, grass, a baseball (Draw them in with markers of various colors, or have a student draw them and mount them on the board, or make them of brightly colored construction paper, fabric, etc.)

Signs

These signs guide you safely on the road.

These signs guide your reading and writing.

SLOW

SPEED LIMIT 50

STOP

NO RIGHT TURN

SINGLE LANE AHEAD

Take One

Be safe! Be smart!
Use them both!

Signs Students often need to be reminded to use a punctuation mark at the end of each sentence. An independent seat-work activity related to punctuation can be mimeographed and tucked into the Take-One pocket of this board. (See example exercise, page 78.)

You'll need:

A lining for the board (light blue)

Cutout letters for the title and slogan at the bottom (dark blue)

Common road signs (Have students draw and cut out the signs in the proper shapes and colors. They may want to observe and copy actual signs, or obtain a pamphlet from the library or the Department of Highways.)

Marks of punctuation (Have the students cut them out in various sizes from construction paper in pinks, oranges, reds.)

A "road sign" (dark-blue marker on white oaktag, mounted on a brown construction-paper "stake")

Grass (Fringe a strip or two of green construction paper and staple it around the bottom of the stake.)

A Take-One folder (dark blue. See instructions, page 11.)

Even a silly sentence has 2 parts!
Subject + Predicate = Sentence

The tiny mouse	wore a red saddle.
The happy stars	turned somersaults.
The little gray pony	howled at the moon.
The circus clown	smiled in the sky.
The big hound dog	was afraid of the cat.

Can you make sense of these?

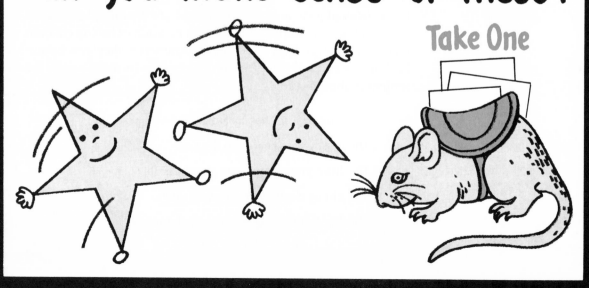

Take One

Subjects and Predicates   This board gives the simple-sentence formula and points up the subject and predicate of five silly sentences. The sentences make sense if the subjects and predicates are rearranged, and this activity further emphasizes their function.

Independent seat-work activities related to sentence structure can be mimeographed and placed in the Take-One pocket. (See sample exercise, page 79.)

You'll need:

A lining for the board (white)

The messages, "Even a silly sentence has 2 parts!" "Subject + Predicate = Sentence" and "Can You Make Sense of These?" (a combination of red, orange, and pink)

Five subjects and five predicates (black marker on orange paper for the subjects, on pink paper for the predicates. The two colors emphasize the two sentence parts.)

A mouse wearing a red saddle, stars turning somersaults, or other figures suggested by the silly sentences (Cut the figures from brightly colored paper. Draw in the features and details with marker.)

A Take-One folder (pink or orange. See instructions, page 11.)

If the five subjects and five predicates are thumbtacked to the board, rather than stapled, a lesson can be made of having children rearrange them so they make sense. Afterward, they can be put back in the original "silly" order for display. To make sense, the sentences should read:

The tiny mouse was afraid of the cat.

The happy stars smiled in the sky.

The little gray pony wore a red saddle.

The circus clown turned somersaults.

The big hound dog howled at the moon.

31

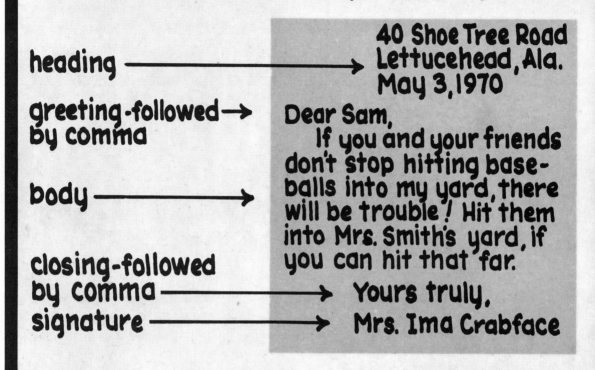

Mrs. Crabface's Friendly Friendly Letter

heading ────────────→ 40 Shoe Tree Road
Lettucehead, Ala.
May 3, 1970

greeting-followed →
by comma

Dear Sam,
    If you and your friends don't stop hitting baseballs into my yard, there will be trouble! Hit them into Mrs. Smith's yard, if you can hit that far.

body ────────────→

closing-followed
by comma ────────────→ Yours truly,
signature ────────────→ Mrs. Ima Crabface

**Mrs. Crabface's
Friendly Friendly Letter**

A sample form of the friendly letter, this bulletin board takes up only a small space and can be a visual aid to students in writing friendly letters throughout the semester or year. If there is room on the board, you might want to add a large sample addressed envelope and post some of the students' finished friendly letters.

A similar board can be made for a sample composition showing margins, heading, title, and indentations.

You'll need:

    A lining for the board (yellow)

    Title, parts of the letter, the letter itself (red marker on pink paper)

Composition

The Story Is in the Bag!

The Story Is in the Bag! This composition topic is designed to stimulate imaginative story writing. Bring in six or eight different kinds of bags. Stuff them with crumpled paper for a 3-D effect. Thumbtack them to the bulletin board and ask students to choose one bag to tell a story about. To help give them ideas, ask these questions:

1. What might be in the bag?
2. How could it have gotten there?
3. Whom does the bag belong to? Who has it now?
4. Did the bag change someone's life?
5. Did anything good or bad happen because of it?
6. Is there a secret about the bag or what's in it?

Here are some types of bags you might use:

a rumpled department-store sack

a department-store shopping bag

a very *small* bag (perhaps from a nut shop)

a laundry bag

a grocery bag

a long Italian- or French-bread sack

a burlap sack

a candy or popcorn bag

Correct the stories and have the students re-copy them. Assemble the bulletin board.

You'll need:

A lining for the board (yellow)

Cutout letters for "The Story Is in the Bag!" (dark green)

The stuffed bags stapled to the board

A few compositions mounted on construction paper (green and orange)

Display only a few compositions at a time, and change them frequently until all the children's stories have been posted. Each child has a special feeling of pride when his story is not lost among thirty other papers.

What makes you _you_ ?

It's how you look at things.

What Makes You You? This board illustrates that each student's personal views help set him apart as an individual.

Ask all the students to write a story about a picture you have selected from a magazine. Choose a large picture with large elements that can be seen by all the students. When the stories are read aloud and mounted, emphasize to the class that although all of the children saw the same picture, each of them created a different story about it. This may motivate a discussion of individuality and the many factors that make people different from each other.

Correct the stories and have the students re-copy them. Then assemble the board.

You'll need:

A lining for the board (white)

The message, "What makes you you?" and "It's how you look at things." (dark-green marker)

The motivating picture (mount it on dark-green construction paper, then mount the whole on paper loops or small cereal boxes to make it stand out. See instructions, page 10.)

A montage of faces (Have students cut them from magazines and paste or staple them up. They may want to include snapshots of themselves.)

A few compositions mounted on construction paper (in several different bright colors)

Display only a few compositions at a time and change them often. With this topic, it's *particularly* important for the children to feel like special individuals!

The Biggest Whoppers!

Whopper List

1. crazy
2. eight
3. asleep
4. marshmallows
5. stole
6. green
7. enormous
8. exactly
9. frightened
10. under

The Biggest Whoppers! A whopper, of course, is a fantastically unbelievable story. There is a "whopper list" of five to ten words, depending on the age and ability of the children. Each word must be included in the whopper composition. For variety, let students choose from two whopper lists. Spelling words may be included.

Correct the compositions and have the students re-copy them. Then assemble the board.

You'll need:

A lining for the board (chartreuse)

Cut out letters for "The Biggest Whoppers!" (hot pink)

Circles of different sizes (hot pink)

A Whopper List (dark-green marker)

A few compositions mounted on construction paper (Match the color of the whopper list.)

Display only a few compositions and change them often.

Mathematics and Science

What's in a Number?

$(100 \div 2) - 40 =$

$109 - 99 =$

$5 + 5 =$

$(9 + 7) - 6 =$

$$\begin{array}{r} 2 \\ 2 \\ 2 \\ 2 \\ + 2 \\ \hline \end{array}$$

$$\begin{array}{r} 3 \\ 1 \\ 4 \\ + 2 \\ \hline \end{array}$$

three plus seven

Take One

$$\begin{array}{r} 25 \\ \times 40 \\ \hline \end{array}$$

All of these numerals, words, pictures, and objects express the same number. Do you know what it is?

What's in a Number? This board introduces a "new math" concept: the difference between a *numeral*, which is a symbol and always written the same way (such as Arabic numeral 5 or Roman numeral V or even the word five), and a *number,* which is an abstract idea and can be written, pictured, demonstrated, pantomimed, or imagined in an infinite number of ways. Ten, of course, is the number this board illustrates, with a string of paper dolls, a school of fish, two hands (ten fingers), a domino, play money, and various combinations of numerals.

An independent seat-work activity related to the board can be mimeographed and tucked into the Take-One pocket. (See sample exercise, page 80.)

You'll need:

A lining for the board (white)

Cutout letters for "What's in a Number?" (black)

The message "All of these numerals . . . (black marker on a pastel paper, or chalk on black paper)

Numerals, words, pictures (Use as many varied materials as you can find, such as corrugated cardboard, colored construction paper, wrapping paper, magazine pages, newspaper, yarn, etc. Use bright, gay colors and varied sizes. Cut fish out of gold-colored paper and draw in waves and bubbles with blue marker. A real domino — showing two fives — can be fastened in place with a small roll of masking tape, sticky side out. Staple on play money adding up to $10. For the ten fingers, have a child draw around his two hands on pink or flesh-colored construction paper.)

A Take-One folder (pastel paper with black lettering. See instructions, page 11.)

What Do We Measure?

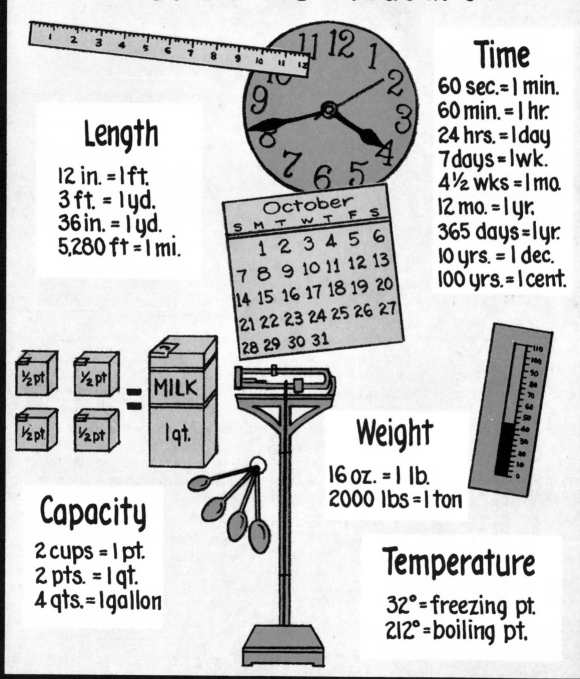

Time

60 sec. = 1 min.
60 min. = 1 hr.
24 hrs. = 1 day
7 days = 1 wk.
4½ wks = 1 mo.
12 mo. = 1 yr.
365 days = 1 yr.
10 yrs. = 1 dec.
100 yrs. = 1 cent.

Length

12 in. = 1 ft.
3 ft. = 1 yd.
36 in. = 1 yd.
5,280 ft = 1 mi.

Weight

16 oz. = 1 lb.
2000 lbs = 1 ton

Capacity

2 cups = 1 pt.
2 pts. = 1 qt.
4 qts. = 1 gallon

Temperature

32° = freezing pt.
212° = boiling pt.

½ pt. ½ pt. ½ pt. ½ pt. = MILK 1 qt.

October
S M T W T F S
1 2 3 4 5 6
7 8 9 10 11 12 13
14 15 16 17 18 19 20
21 22 23 24 25 26 27
28 29 30 31

What Do We Measure? Both children and adults tend to equate measurement with linear measurement. This board stretches the concept of measurement to include weight, temperature, time, and capacity and may encourage the class to think of other types of measurement such as barometric pressure, or combined measurements such as speed in miles-per-hour, light in foot-candles, acceleration in feet-per-second-per-second, or even Einstein's $e = mc^2$. Whenever the class talks of a measurement — in math, science, space studies, sports, current events — they may want to decide what category the measurement falls into. The tables of measurement on the board serve as a useful daily reminder to students learning the basic measurements.

You'll need:

A lining for the board (a pastel, such as yellow)

Cutout letters for "What Do We Measure?" (green)

The tables of measurement (navy marker on white paper)

Yardstick, tape measure, milk cartons, measuring spoons, calendar, and play watch (Have students collect them.)

Scale, clock face, and thermometer (Make these, or have a student make them, out of construction paper or oaktag.)

Two daily activities can be centered around the board. A student can mark off each day on the calendar. And the day's temperature (or predicted high temperature) can be recorded on the thermometer if it is made this way:

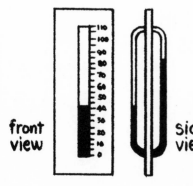

front view   side view

1. Mark off degrees on a strip of white oaktag.
2. Cut slots at top and bottom.
3. Make a loop of ribbon just long enough to thread through the slots — half red ribbon and half white ribbon.
4. Mark the day's temperature by pulling the red ribbon up or down to the proper degree.

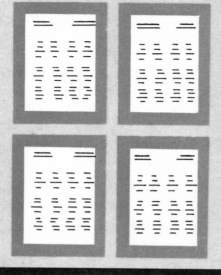

Arithmetic

If you ask your mother for one fried egg for breakfast and she gives you two fried eggs and you eat both of them who is better at arithmetic, you or your mother?

-from "Arithmetic" by Carl Sandburg

Arithmetic   This board provides a simple but interesting display area for children's math papers. The poem "Arithmetic" by Carl Sandburg gives a funny, child's view of arithmetic. You may want to read the entire poem to the class or mimeograph copies for them to keep. It can motivate a discussion of ways arithmetic is involved in their own lives, and they may even enjoy writing their own versions of "Arithmetic."*

You'll need:

A lining for the board (yellow)

Cutout letters for "Arithmetic" or "Mathematics" if you prefer (orange)

A few students' papers mounted on construction paper (orange)

Change the students' papers often, and the same basic display can serve for a number of weeks.

*The complete poem "Arithmetic" by Carl Sandburg appears in *Reflections on a Gift of Watermelon Pickle, and in the Arrow Book of Funny Poems,* both available from Scholastic Book Services.

Great Men   This board can easily be changed to illustrate a series of different discoveries and accomplishments. Some alternatives might be: a candle and an electric light; a needle and thread and a sewing machine; the Tom Thumb and a modern monorail train; a primitive plow and a modern cultivator; a stethoscope and a news photo of a heart-transplant patient. The class may enjoy thinking up and illustrating new combinations themselves.

You'll need:

A lining for the board (red)

The titles (navy or black marker)

A balloon and a Saturn rocket (Make the strings for the balloon of yarn. Use the cardboard tube from a roll of paper towels as a base for the rocket, and fluffy cotton for steam and clouds.)

We Have a Secret!   The secret of the fruits and vegetables? Not only are they delicious, they are good for you too. The board and the light poem mimeographed and tucked into the Take-One pocket can motivate or supplement a science or health lesson on food values.

You'll need:

A lining for the board (white)

A "conversation balloon" (green marker on white or light-green paper)

Fruits and vegetables (Have students make them of colored construction paper.)

A Take-One folder (green construction paper. See instructions, page 11.)

WE HAVE A SECRET

We have a little secret
That we hesitate to tell:
Not only do we taste good,
We have vitamins as well!

So eat us fruits and vegetables.
Eat us every day.
For it really is no secret
That we keep bad health away!

The Miss Planet Contest

Poor Earth. She didn't win one award. Jupiter wins for being the biggest. Mercury wins the "Smallest Planet" title. Saturn with her beautiful rings wins for being the fanciest.

Oh well, we'll give her honorable mention for being the friendliest. A friendly planet? Yes! 3 reasons why!

The Miss Planet Contest   This contest points out the popular distinctions of some of the planets, but primarily emphasizes the reasons why human life survives on the earth.

You'll need:

A lining for the board (white)

Cutout letters for "The Miss Planet Contest" (dark blue)

The message, "Poor Earth . . ." (navy marker on white paper)

Three flaps with printed or typed "reasons" underneath (dark-blue paper with numbers cut from white paper)

Earth (green or blue paper. Drawing in the North American continent helps identify it as Earth.)

Honorable Mention scroll (navy marker on white paper)

A few stars, covered with glitter

reason number one: Earth is just the right distance from the sun. Nearer to the sun and we would be too hot. Farther from the sun and we would be too cold. Our distance from the sun helps make Earth the planet most friendly to human life.

reason number two: Earth's atmosphere is friendly, too. It has oxygen for animals and carbon dioxide for plants. It keeps out harmful radiations from the sun, but lets in plenty of heat and light. At night, when we are turned away from the sun, the atmosphere acts as a blanket, holding in enough heat to keep us warm.

Without Earth's atmosphere, we could not breathe or eat. And we would burn by day and freeze by night!

reason number three: Earth's oceans, seas, lakes, and rivers are also our friends. Plants and animals cannot live without water, and no other planet has as much water as Earth.

Earth may not be the biggest or the smallest or the fanciest. But she certainly wins as the friendliest!

Thanks, plants

Thanks, Plants   This board is an easy way to motivate a unit on plants. The unit might deal with food and other plant products, and the oxygen-carbon dioxide exchange between plants and animals. A class scribe might keep a list of things for which we are grateful to plants and post it on the bulletin board.

You'll need:

     A lining for the board (a pastel)

     Cutout letters for "Thanks, Plants" (green)

     Plants, leaves, flowers (Collect as many kinds as possible: real greenery, paper and plastic flowers, magazine pictures.)

Social
Studies

Pioneers Go West

These are the necessary foods for a 5 month trip by covered wagon from Missouri to Oregon for just one family.

600 lbs. flour
100 lbs. sugar
300 lbs. smoked meats
30 lbs. coffee
25 lbs. salt
180 lbs. dried fruit
30 lbs. dried beans

3 kegs vinegar
20 lbs. corn meal
spices
molasses
pepper
raisins

salt

sugar

corn meal

flour

Pioneers Go West　This list of the quantities and kinds of food a pioneer family needed for a month-long trip is a detail that will lend reality to a unit on pioneer life.

You'll need:

A lining for the board (white)

Cutout letters for "Pioneers Go West" (brown)

The provisions list and the message, "These are the necessary foods. . ." (brown marker)

Outline of a large covered wagon (Have a student draw it in orange, or outline it in yarn.)

Product containers (Have students collect. Emphasize to the class that the pioneers didn't have the convenience of such containers. You may prefer to have the children make bags and label them. If so, stuff the bags with paper for a 3-D effect.)

Our Favorite

Sports Story

Home Town Boys Win Championship

Jim D.

Tony

Joe P.

Alice A

Tom

Suzanne S.

Sara and Mary

This Week

Our Favorite Story
This Week

Here is a board that motivates both current events and reading lessons. News reading becomes a game when students try to find a "winning" story in a given category. The various sections of a newspaper are introduced as they search each week for an interesting sports story, front page story, foreign-national-or-local news story, editorial, letter to the editor, editorial cartoon, "human interest" story, society page story, movie or TV industry story — or even a favorite comic strip!

Let the class vote on the most interesting story in the week's category and post it in the "winner's box."

Another reading skill (finding the main idea) can be painlessly worked in by cutting off the story's headline and having the class make up headlines and vote for the best one — the one that most vividly sums up the main point of the story.

You'll need:

A lining for the board (white)

Cutout letters for "Our Favorite" and "This Week" (red)

The week's category, such as "Sports Story" (red marker on a strip of white paper — it's easy to change each week)

A "winner's box" (Mount the winning story on construction paper and staple it to a small cereal box or paper rings to make it stand away from the board.)

The winning headline (Print it on a strip of white paper and staple it above the winner's box.)

The other articles submitted (Mount them on pieces of red construction paper and print the name or names of the children who submitted them in black marker.)

Each week, change the category, headline, and news articles.

Each Part Does Its Part

Alaska

Hawaii

Each Part Does Its Part Students often see product maps in two dimensions. By using real items made from the raw products, the board becomes more exciting. Students can bring in items to add to the map as successive parts of the country are studied.

You'll need:

A lining for the board (white)

Cutout letters for "Each Part Does Its Part" (dark blue)

A large outline map of the United States (See instructions for making your own, page 12.)

Some Sectional Industries and Products

Northeast

ship building (toy boat); lumber and paper (pencil, paper handkerchief); fish (frozen-fish wrapper); berries (frozen-berry wrapper); chemicals (toy test tube); clothing (doll's dress); textiles (fabric swatch); machinery (toy machine); coal (small lump of coal); dairy products (cheese wrapper); maple syrup (syrup label); shoes (doll shoe)

South

cotton (fluffy cotton); tobacco (candy cigarette); citrus fruits (orange-juice label); peaches (peach-can label); coal (small lump of coal); sugar (tiny sugar packet); petroleum (petroleum jelly label); textiles (fabric swatch); lumber (popsicle stick)

Midwest

lumber (toothpick); furniture (doll furniture); wheat and corn (small cereal box); iron and steel (nail); automobiles (toy car); dairy products (butter wrapper); gold (crumpled gold foil)

Southwest

copper (penny); lumber (tongue depresser); paper (small pad); beef cattle (toy steer); petroleum (toy oil can)

Far West

lumber (twig); oranges (orange-juice label); apples (applesauce label); potatoes (instant-potato box); grapes (plastic grape or grape-juice label); fish (frozen-fish wrapper); oil (small can of sewing-machine oil); copper (penny); silver (crumpled silver foil); lead (paint-can label)

Alaska

fur (tiny piece of fur); fish (frozen-fish wrapper)

Hawaii

pineapple (pineapple-can label)

Don't blame girls for talking so much.

Samuel F. B. Morse invented the telegraph in 1844, and soon a girl could send a birthday wire to her Aunt Min in Minnesota!

In 1876, Alexander Graham Bell invented the telephone. Girls certainly learned how to use that invention fast!

Satellites such as Telstar One, launched in 1962, bring us live TV shows from all over the world. How long will it be before girls learn to use this new way to communicate!

It's the boys' fault for inventing such easy ways to communicate.

Communications   This board provides a humorous motivation for a communications unit.

You'll need:

A lining for the board (yellow))

The messages (black marker on white paper. Top and bottom lines can be lettered directly on the lining.)

Telegraph, telephone, Telstar satellite (Have students make these of construction paper.)

A "wire" (Use black yarn.)

58

Poetry... and Others

HOW TO EAT A POEM

Don't be polite.
Bite in.
Pick it up with your fingers and lick the juice that may run down
   your chin.
It is ready and ripe now, whenever you are.

You do not need a knife or fork or spoon or plate or napkin or
tablecloth.

For there is no core
or stem
or rind
or pit
or seed
or skin
to throw away.

Eve Merriam

60

How to Eat a Poem   "How to Eat a Poem" by Eve Merriam is a charming poem. Its message: Don't stand in awe of poetry. Just enjoy it! Mimeograph "How to Eat a Poem" and tuck it into a Take-One pocket for all the children to keep and enjoy.

You'll need:

A lining for the board (pink)

Cutout letters for "How to Eat a Poem" (dark blue)

"by Eve Merriam," "Don't be polite. Bite in." and "Some Delicious Poems" (red and blue markers)

A boy eating a poem (Draw him yourself or have a student draw him.)

A Take-One folder (blue with dark-blue cutout letters. See instructions, page 11.)

A few short poems mounted on construction paper (Try some short poems from your language-arts books. Use orange paper.)

Strips to divide the board in half (one of blue, one of orange)

Falling-from-a-Tree Poems

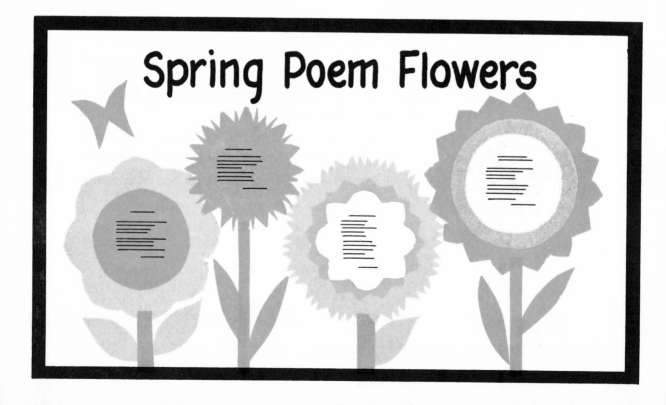

Spring Poem Flowers

Here are two seasonal boards for displaying the students' own poetry. Have each student print his poem on a leaf or flower center. Change the poems on the board often so each child feels his poem is special. The poems do not have to be about fall or spring.

Falling-from-a-Tree Poems

You'll need:

A lining for the board (brown)

A tree cut from construction paper (white)

Leaves (Have each child cut his own leaf from white or orange paper and print his poem directly on it. Cut a few decorative leaves in the same colors.)

Cutout letters for "Falling-from-a-Tree Poems" (orange)

Spring Poem Flowers

You'll need:

A lining for the board (white)

"Spring Poem Flowers" (green marker)

Four large flowers (Cut them from orange, pink, yellow, and blue paper with green stems).

Flower centers (Have each child cut a flower center from a pattern in a pastel paper and print his poem directly on it.)

A bluebird or butterfly (Have a student cut one from construction paper.)

And you thought crayons were just for coloring!

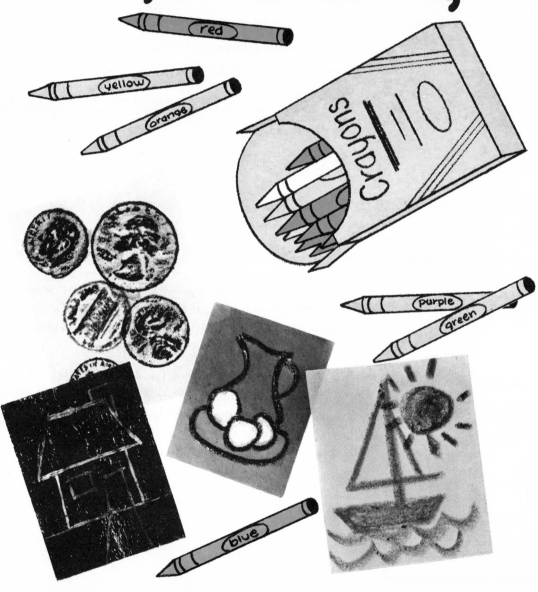

Crayon Art Crayons are the most common art material in the elementary classroom; but teachers and students are often surprised to learn how many art techniques are possible with crayons.

You'll need:

A lining for the board (white)

The message, "And you thought. . ." (dark-blue marker)

A giant crayon box (Cover a small dress box with white or brown paper and draw the front of a familiar crayon box on it.)

Giant crayons (Roll up different colors of construction paper. Cut points at one end with scissors. Draw a "wrapper" on each.)

The children's crayon art (Change both the crayon technique on display and the individual drawings often.)

Here are some crayon techniques the children will love!

crayon resist Draw a picture or a design with crayons. Press fairly hard on the crayon so the lines are dark and waxy. Fill in the lines with watercolor paint — or just paint over the whole drawing. The crayon will show through because it repels or resists water. Finger paints can also be used. Non-absorbent paper such as finger-paint paper or shelf paper is best.

checkerboard drawings Make a checkerboard effect with white or yellow crayon. Draw a picture or design over it with the same crayon. Fill in the picture squares with the cool watercolors — blue, green, purple. Fill in the background squares with the hot colors — red, pink, orange. Use non-absorbent paper.

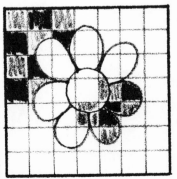

crayon etching   Fill a paper with crayoned squares of different bright colors. Then color black over everything. Draw or etch into the black crayon with scissors or a straight pen and brightly colored lines will appear from underneath.

crayon rubbing   Put a leaf under a thin sheet of paper. Rub the crayon over it and the leaf pattern will be brought out. Also rub over scissors, a comb, coins, oaktag cutouts, or other interesting objects. Collage effects can be made with small, flat objects.

transparent overlapping   Draw three bottles or other simple shapes overlapping each other. Crayon each bottle in one of the primary colors — red, blue, yellow. Secondary colors will appear in the overlap.

stained glass   The effect of stained glass can be obtained by shaving crayon between sheets of waxed paper and ironing it with a warm iron. The designs produced are colorful and long-lasting. They are particularly beautiful when taped to a windowpane to let light shine through.

transparent overlapping

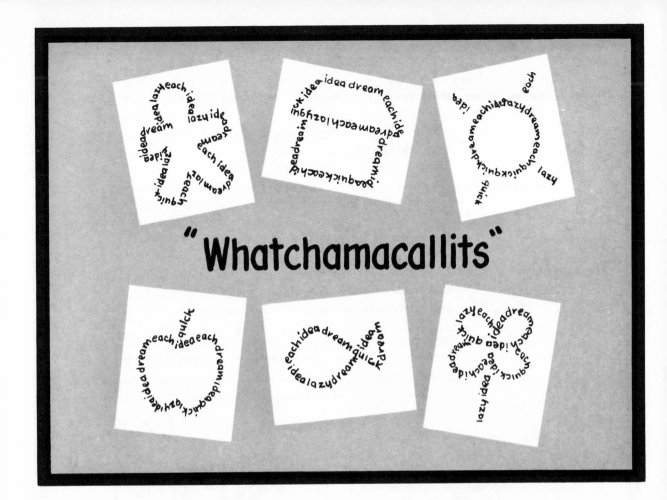

Whatchamacallits

"Whatchamacallits" can make spelling practice fun. Students make drawings, but they are not permitted to use plain lines — only words written side-by-side to form lines. Write the spelling list on the blackboard. Let the students choose colored construction paper. Let them draw whatever they like using the spelling words as "lines." Each word must be written five times — but children usually have such fun with whatchamacallits that they voluntarily write each word more than five times.

You'll need:

A lining for the board (yellow)

Cutout letters for "Whatchamacallits" (orange)

The students' "Whatchamacallits"

Does School give you the Z-Z-Z's ?

If so, it's time to have a "Stamp Out the Z-Z-Z's Talk" with Mrs Cox.

Suggestions

The Z-Z-Z's In midyear, this board can give a lift to classroom routine. It offers a chance for student-teacher planning, and encourages lively classroom discussions about classroom procedures.

Post the board and suggestion box at the beginning of the week. Discuss the kinds of suggestions the students might put in the box — ideas about new things they want to learn, student participation in learning, a different schedule, trips, or projects.

At the end of a designated period, take down the suggestion box and read over the suggestions. The ones that suggest longer lunch and play periods can be treated with humor. The serious ones can be discussed by the class. Some real changes should result from the discussion. The experience can be pointed up as an example of democratic planning.

You'll need:

A lining for the board (yellow)

Cutout letters for "Z-Z-Z's" (black)

The rest of the message (black marker)

A shoe box marked "Suggestions" (Cover the box with attractive paper.)

Four cartoons (Draw them yourself or have a student copy them.)

Hygiene Ha-Ha's

Hygiene Ha-Ha's Humor is easier to swallow than instruction. So try these silly rhymes to teach some rules of cleanliness and hygiene.

You'll need:

A lining for the board (light blue)

Cutout letters for "Hygiene Ha-Ha's" (red)

The rhymes (print them with black marker on white paper, and mount them on red.)

A comb, a washcloth, a toothbrush, and empty boxes of tissues, bath soap, shampoo, detergent, and cotton-tipped swabs

Post these jingles next to the items on the board — or make up your own!

comb: Brush and comb hair often.
It is the modern trend.
Besides, it's good insurance that
A gorilla won't be your friend.

toothbrush: "Do you use toothpaste to brush your teeth?"
I asked wise Mrs. Dare.
"What else?" replied the dear old soul,
"Would I use it to brush my hair?"

soap: Before I rob Mom's cookie jar
I wash my hands and rinse.
I don't care about killing germs,
But I hate to leave fingerprints!

cotton-tipped swabs: How many years
Since you've had clean ears?

detergent: I'm joining in the space-age race,
So I wear clean clothes —— just in case
I'm asked to take the honored place
Of greeting guests from outer space!

tissues: Tissues are light and fly in the breeze.
They're friends and pals whenever you sneeze!

shampoo: Shampoo?
Do!

washcloth: Take a bath regularly.
It's not hard to do.
It will keep you smelling fresh
And keep your tub clean, too!

What's So Great About TV?

What's So Great About TV? This board can help you encourage the students to develop judgment and discernment about TV shows. The children may even enjoy knowing that they are learning things and broadening their vocabularies while having fun watching TV.

You'll need:

A lining for the board (Cover it with several television pages from the newspapers.)

Cutout letters for "What's So Great About TV?" (dark green)

A TV set (black marker on brown and white construction paper)

Pictures of popular TV stars (Have the students bring them in.)

TV questionnaires mounted on construction paper (dark green)

Later, you may want to replace the questionnaires with compositions the students write about TV programs.

TV Questionnaire The TV questionnaire might include these questions for the class to answer:

1. Name three of your favorite TV programs.
2. Name three TV programs you do <u>not</u> like.
3. Tell why you like one TV program.
4. Tell why you do <u>not</u> like one TV program.
5. Tell three facts you learned from watching TV.
6. Name and define three words you learned from watching TV.

Our Wish for the World
This board is especially appealing because each child sees his hand in the word "peace." As a homework assignment, tell children to choose any kind of paper they like — colored construction paper, newspaper, a magazine page, an old homework paper, a paper bag, wrapping paper — trace their hands on it and cut them out. The student's choice of paper will reflect his personality and add to the board's appeal.

You'll need:

A lining for the board (silver wrapping paper)

Cutout letters for "Our Wish for the World" (glossy red paper)

Cutout hands to form the word "PEACE" (About 60 hands are needed, so each child should cut at least two.)

If the board is used at the Christmas and Hanukkah season, bits of holly and tinsel will enhance it.

"Take One"
--Some
Samples

Contractions
(See pp. 22-23)

Study Guide: 10 common contractions

isn't = is not	aren't = are not
can't = can not	it's = it is
won't = will not	I've = I have
don't = do not	they're = they are
shouldn't = should not	I'm = I am

Self-quiz. Replace words in parentheses with contractions.

1. (I am) not going to forget contractions.

2. (It is) so easy to learn them. I (should not) make any mistakes.

3. (They are) much easier than fractions.

4. I (can not) wait to check these. I bet (I have) gotten 100 per cent.

5. Apostrophes (are not) tadpoles.

6. (They are) alike in looks, though.

7. (Would not) it be silly to use a tadpole instead of a contraction?

8. I bet Mrs. (teacher) (can not) stand tadpoles.

9. I (do not) know what she would do if I put a tadpole on her desk.

10. She (will not) be very happy if I do that.

11. The word "contraction" (is not) hard to spell.

Homonyms
(See pp. 24-25)

Learn the Horrible Homonyms

Homonyms sound alike but have different spellings and meanings.

     they're — they are (contraction)
     their — belonging
     there — in that place

Fill in each blank in the story with one of the above homonyms.

    The homymonsters are walking to ———— home. ———— going very slowly. They live over ————. When they get ———— they will eat soup. ———— favorite soup is mushroom soup. ———— stand those homymonsters who love mushroom soup! ———— able to eat five bowls of soup. ———— mother makes such delicious mushroom soup! ———— is the homymonsters' mother, making mushroom soup.

     your — belonging to you
     you're — you are (contraction)

Fill in each blank with one of the above homonyms.

    ———— not eating ———— soup. I bet ———— soup is not as good as the homymonsters' soup. If ———— not going to eat it, can I? ———— right! The homymonsters' soup is better than ———— soup.

Directions: This story has no punctuation marks at the ends of sentences. Read the story and put in the correct marks. Use a period for a statement, a question mark for a question, and an exclamation point for an exclamation. You should use 4 question marks, about 17 periods and about 3 exclamation points. Many sentences may take either a period or an exclamation point; you may use more than 3 exclamation points and fewer than 17 periods.

The Three-Dozen-Cookie Tummyache

When George Harris got home from school, he saw cookies on the table   They were homemade chocolate chip cookies   Wow   Were they his favorite   Of course they were   Susie said to wait until their mother came home before eating them   Did George wait   Of course he didn't   In ten minutes he ate thirty-six   That makes three dozen

When Mrs. Harris came home she looked at the table   The table was there but the cookies weren't   George's mother knew where those cookies were   They were inside George   But where was George

George's mother looked out the window and saw George playing baseball   He was way out in left field   The ball was hit far past him   He tried to catch it, but he could barely run   The batter got a home run   George got a three-dozen-cookie tummyache   Mrs. Harris got some satisfaction   She thought George would never eat thirty-six cookies again   Do you think she was right

Subjects and Predicates
(See pp. 30-31)

Draw lines to connect the right subject and predicate.

1.	The old man	A.	played basketball last Tuesday.
2.	My kitten	B.	bounced off the wall.
3.	A red ball	C.	walked with a cane.
4.	This leaf	D.	licked up the milk on the floor.
5.	I	E.	turned red when autumn came.

Write your own predicates to complete the sentences below:

Subject	Predicate (write your own)
1. Mary Jones	_____
2. My favorite TV star	_____
3. Many circus clowns	_____
4. Red and white candy canes	_____
5. His cousin's grandfather's brother	_____

Write your own subjects to begin the sentences below:

Subject (write your own)	Predicate
1. _____	comes from outer space!
2. _____	hit me in the face with a pie.
3. _____	only flies at night.
4. _____	will run the mile in four minutes.
5. _____	grows in gardens.

Numbers
(See pp. 40-41)

1. All but two of these numeral-combinations express the number 15.

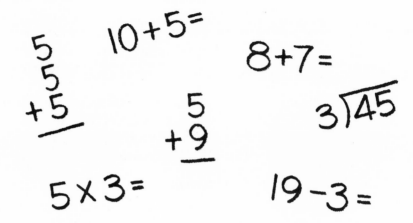

$$\begin{array}{r} 5 \\ 5 \\ +5 \\ \hline \end{array}$$

$$10+5=$$

$$8+7=$$

$$3\overline{)45}$$

$$\begin{array}{r} 5 \\ +9 \\ \hline \end{array}$$

$$5\times3=$$

$$19-3=$$

Which two numeral-combinations do <u>not</u> express 15? _____

_____

2. Pick a number between 1 and 100. Write it here: _____
Express the number you picked in at least ten different ways.

(Leave plenty of space.)